I0879152

ABANDONED KANSAS CITY

REGINA DANIEL

AMERICA THROUGH TIME®
ADDING COLOR TO AMERICAN HISTORY

America Through Time is an imprint of Fonthill Media LLC
www.through-time.com
office@through-time.com

Published by Arcadia Publishing by arrangement with Fonthill Media LLC
For all general information, please contact Arcadia Publishing:
Telephone: 843-853-2070
Fax: 843-853-0044
E-mail: sales@arcadiapublishing.com
For customer service and orders:
Toll-Free 1-888-313-2665

www.arcadiapublishing.com

First published 2019

ISBN 978-1-63499-162-9

Typeset in Trade Gothic 10pt on 15pt
Printed and bound in England

CONTENTS

DEDICATION

This book is dedicated to all my supporters along the way, the partners that ventured into danger with me, my family for being awesome, Joe Lynch for putting my doubt to rest, and most of all, Christopher. Each one of you had a special role in making this dream a reality.

INTRODUCTION

Being an urban explorer is a lot like being a tourist, but in your own city. Most of the time, it is the bad parts of the city. For many reasons, I have personal rules and ethics that I stick to when venturing out. After a decent amount of research, I never go alone, and I never break in. The places that I photograph are in different stages of decay; however, I am a photographer, not a vandal. It is my goal to leave it as I found it.

After learning the where, when, and how of each place I photograph, I still feel like I'm discovering something new every time I go out. Off the beaten path and tucked away into neighborhoods I've never visited, I photograph places that much of the city forgets is there. Some places are preserved like a time capsule with the books, papers, and other objects still sitting where they were left, while others are only a memory of what they used to be. Each place has its own story to tell as to why it's abandoned, such as structural integrity, declining enrollment, or logistical growth. These reasons are only the beginning.

One of the twenty apartment buildings boarded up at the Chouteau Court complex.

Within abandoned Kansas City, there is so much to offer. There are many churches, hotels, businesses, and schools to choose from. Occasionally, an unusual place comes along. Of those places, I have gotten to explore a hospital, race track, drive-in, waterslide, juvenile detention facility, neighborhood reservoir, a couple of tunnels, apartment complexes, and a historic jail designed as a castle.

Above: Vines almost cover the side of the original part of the small hospital at Wheatley-Provident Hospital.

Right: Start/Finish line from the flag platform at the I-70 Speedway.

One of the four screens at the I-70 Drive-In.

Unable to locate any information about this waterslide, I took to social media in search of anyone who could give me some history. The responses came flooding in from those who spent summer days either working or having fun there. The details are a bit hazy, but it was established that it was Peppy's Slip & Slide. It was opened in the 1978-1979 timeframe and eventually closed sometime between 1984 or 1985.

View through a torn screen from the main building at McCune Residential Center. This facility was for troubled boys, ages thirteen to seventeen.

Side walkway looking into the reservoir.

Above left: Vale Tunnel. Opened in 1904. This tunnel was one of four that would be part of the Rock Island railroad that closed in 1980 due to financial issues. Located under Bannister Road.

Above right: Side porch and the larger turret of the work castle.

Part of Rosedale Ridge Apartments. Photo taken December 2017.

1

GREENWOOD AND MARLBOROUGH

I have been through many empty schools. They are probably the buildings that I explore and photograph the most. All of them are like the proverbial snowflakes—no two are alike. Each has its own unique design and layouts. Even though there are plenty to choose from, each one is a whole new experience.

I remember my first school like it was yesterday. After much research, I had a full list of places to explore, starting with Greenwood Elementary. This school shares a corner with Kansas City's first underground pedestrian crossings. Built in 1906, the three-story school is boarded up all around on the ground level, except one of the back doors, where someone had previously made an easy way in.

Stepping in, my adrenaline began to flow. My partner and I clicked on our lights, but it didn't make much of a difference. The pitch black enveloped everything, including our hands in front of our faces. I remember being terrified of walking into a questionable darkness, but once I pushed beyond my fear, a school hallway revealed itself, after being closed off to the world since 1997.

The climbing ropes still hung in the gymnasium, the manual pencil sharpeners were still on the walls, and the red curtains still adorned the auditorium stage; however, all of this was just left to deteriorate. The third floor of the 100-plus-year-old school was collapsing into the floor below. Despite neighborhood efforts to save the school, it was demolished in late 2018.

Front entrance to Greenwood Elementary.

Away from the view of the street, the back entrance to Greenwood Elementary is tucked away in an architectural alcove.

Right: Staircase in Greenwood Elementary.

Below: Balcony view of the auditorium stage in Greenwood Elementary.

Outside entrance to auditorium at Greenwood Elementary.

Third-floor classroom collapsing into classroom below in Greenwood Elementary.

Unlike my first school, the most recent school I explored wasn't open at all. Boarded up good, I watched Marlborough Elementary for a year, waiting for someone to make a way in.

Built in 1927, the three-story school has sat vacant since 2007. There is a lot of damage throughout the building—not from vandals, but from years of water leaks. As we walked over mushy ceiling tiles and around hanging ceiling parts, we found one hallway was covered with a dinosaur mural. It was satisfying to see the mural in good condition despite the surrounding damage. The auditorium was the real find. There was little damage to the stage and first few rows of seating. I imagine the auditorium looked similar to how it looked the day the school closed over a decade ago. And, like almost every school I have been in, the climbing ropes were still hanging in the gym. Marlborough has recently been purchased, with plans of converting it into apartments and a community garden.

Front entrance to Marlborough Elementary.

Auditorium of Marlborough Elementary.

Auditorium seating at Marlborough Elementary.

Dinosaur mural in the hallway at Marlborough Elementary.

Library at Marlborough Elementary.

After having a few locations under my belt, I found myself wanting to know more about the places I was photographing. Researching the history gave substance to these now empty buildings. Good or bad, all these schools, hotels, churches, and work places meant something to so many people. Right then, that's when being an urban explorer became more than just finding the way in and marking it off my list. I wanted to preserve some of the last known images of what makes up abandoned Kansas City. Once these buildings are gone, they will only exist in our memories. All these places are similar to the toys from our childhood—we grow up eventually leaving them in the past. These buildings were outgrown and left for newer pursuits.

Each location was once full of life. Classrooms were full of children learning from teachers eager to change to world. Working-class individuals punched time clocks, day in and out, to achieve comfort and happiness. Now all those places sit empty with the wind whistling through broken windows, waiting for their next chance to serve a purpose, or else face the chopping block.

Row of town homes at Chouteau Court Apartments. Last resident moved out in January 2018. Residents were relocated for newer accommodations.

Classroom at Paul Robeson Middle School. This was one of the least damaged classrooms.

Vines grow up the rusted tower inside the Northeast Reservoir.

Entrance to the I-70 Drive-In. Closed in September 2018.

Library left full of books at the closed Universal Academy Islamic School.

Located in the West Bottoms, this building is referred to as "The Lab" by local urban explorers.

2

ROSEDALE RIDGE APARTMENTS

When I write about how these places were so full of life, Rosedale Ridge Apartments is one of the first places that comes to mind. The complex was built in 1971. The history of the complex would unfold to a sad or happy ending for its 350 residents, depending on who you ask; some were sad to leave their longtime homes and other were happy for a new start.

Numerous maintenance issues and failing code inspections mounted for a long time. The complaints of black mold, rats, and bed bug infestations that fell on the deaf ears of the complex management forced the county government to step in for the safety of the residents in the spring of 2015. Conditions were so bad that residents only had thirty days to relocate. Even after the complex was abandoned in the summer of 2015, the problems did not stop. Nine months later, one of the buildings had the front facade blown off due to an explosion from a gas leak. The damage was so extensive, the building had to be torn down. Today, the apartment complex is one building less and completely boarded up with brightly colored city notices on all the buildings.

Timing was on my side in December 2017. Someone had made a way into two buildings. Exploring what we could, there were still signs of life throughout many of the apartments. Canned goods in kitchen cabinets, toys and movies scattered up and down the halls, and lots of furniture that nobody wanted to take—all were left behind in everyone's haste of finding a new place to live. I had a very uneasy feeling walking through the complex. All the doors of the building we went into were open except the last two doors at the end of the hall on the third floor. Seeing only those two doors closed and partially blocked with furniture didn't give me a good feeling.

Building 2103 at Rosedale Ridge Apartments.

Second-floor hallway lit up from open apartments at Rosedale Ridge.

Half of the building torn down after a natural gas explosion that occurred in April 2016 at Rosedale Ridge apartments.

We decided to leave without disturbing that end of the hall. The uncomfortable feeling was with me the whole time we were there. It was unusually quiet, except for the sounds of Venetian blinds ratting through broken windows and chirping smoke detectors. Even though most of the building were boarded up, I still felt like we were being watched as we walked around the courtyard. There are so many windows around us, that even if we were really being watched, it would be hard to tell where they would be watching us from. Having spent time here as a kid with friends from elementary school, I still remember what it looked like in 1985, with kids running all over the courtyard and going building to building playing hide and seek. Now, Rosedale Ridge is only a vague recollection of what it was back in the day.

Part of Rosedale Ridge Apartments. Photo taken December 2017.

Throughout my photo journey of abandoned Kansas City, I have had the pleasure of speaking to a few people that either lived, worked, or went to school at the places I have photographed. Hearing their personal stories has so much more levity than any old news article could ever report. Here it was, first-hand experiences from the boy that spent a few years in an isolated juvenile detention facility, the pre-teen girl that roamed the halls of her middle school, and the young mother of two boys getting an apartment big enough for all of them. As they tell me about some of their experiences at these places in their heyday, I couldn't help but envision the people from their stories in my photos.

3

THE EIGHTH STREET TUNNEL

One of the individuals I had the privilege of meeting was Ray Elder, historian for the Kansas City Fire and Historical Society. He grew up in Kansas City and has been the historical guide for tours of the Eighth Street Tunnel.

Located downtown, the tunnel was operational beginning in 1904 until 1956. After the failure of the Ninth Street Incline, the Eighth Street Tunnel was the second project that was engineered to transport people down to the West Bottoms and over into Kansas City. As cars became more readily available, the increasing population of car owners eventually led to the closing of the streetcar and Eighth Street Tunnel. The tunnel would go on to be forgotten about until construction for a new office building started in the 1990s. Since its discovery, a few tours have been offered. I was fortunate enough to get a tour and see a part of the city that was abandoned, buried, and forgotten.

When we got to the door to enter the tunnel, I felt like one of the kids awaiting to enter Willy Wonka's chocolate factory. The brick tunnel went for a few blocks before it disappeared into the darkness. We were only allowed to walk to a certain point—beyond that, the tunnel was becoming structurally dangerous. As we walked, Ray gave us all a very insightful streetcar and Kansas City history lesson. Looking around, you can see stalactites of all lengths hanging from the top of the tunnel. We all left the tunnel glistening from the thick humidity. Ray's tour was so much more than historical facts. He also told the group about his personal experiences riding the streetcar through the tunnel when he was a kid. He even made all of us tour books that included copies of historical photos from his own personal collection.

Office building basement door to enter into the Eighth Street Tunnel.

Water dripping down the wall of the Eighth Street Tunnel.

Eighth Street Tunnel. Photo taken September 2016.

Even though it was a guided tour, I consider the Eighth Tunnel to be my crowning achievement. This is one of the rare occasions where going through the proper channels is completely necessary. The entrance is in the basement of an office building, so trespassing isn't an option.

4

MCCUNE RESIDENTIAL CENTER

This next place, I went in knowing a little history. McCune Residential Center was established in 1908 as McCune Farm for Boys. Named after Jackson County's first juvenile judge, he started the farm as an alternative to jail. Over the years it would change names to McCune Residential Center.

The center provided aid and housing to troubled boys, ages thirteen to seventeen. The center would be closed in 2012, due to funding. The remaining boys were sent to surrounding facilities.

Only empty for a few years when I photographed McCune, there was a lot of ground to cover. There were four housing units, an education building, and a main building, and the whole facility was in very good condition. Besides some ceiling damage and broken windows, many of the cells were still locked, keeping them in the same condition as the day they were closed. The murals on the wall were still bright in color. Motivational materials still even hung on a couple of the walls. I think being in a rural location and surrounded by trees has kept the campus in its current good condition. You wouldn't know it was there unless you were looking for it.

It was a short time later when a local man told me about his time there in the 1980s. He asked me if I found the building in the trees. His question prompted some historical research and a return trip. Just outside the current fence line in a small forested area was a stone structure.

Mural peeling off school lockers at McCune Residential Center for boys.

Damaged ceiling in mural hallway at McCune Residential Center.

Right: Hallway of numbered cells at McCune Residential Center.

Below: Gymnasium in the main center building at McCune Residential Center.

View through broken window from the guard's control room at McCune Residential Center.

One of the original buildings when McCune was a work farm. Located down the hill from the current campus. Built in 1909.

This building was constructed in July 1909. The six-room building was built to house 225 boys. Over a century later, covered in vines and trees, there was this huge stone building with no roof. The hallway was long with two rooms off to each side until the end of the hall, where the last two rooms were next to each other. The stone and mortar walls were all at least fifteen feet high. It was easy to imagine rows of bunks filled with young troubled boys.

Looking back over all the places I have had the opportunity to explore, more and more of them are disappearing due to a myriad of reasons, such as fires, unstable structures, and demolition efforts made by local government. It is always a bit sad to see that a place I took time to research and preserve is now gone, not because I necessarily had an attachment to that place, but because the past has faded away.

Left: Hallway of the six-room building to house 225 boys. Part of the original work farm, this building was built shortly after the farm was established.

Below: Original farm housing for boys, hidden in the trees. I only located this structure with help from a local man that spent time here as a teenager in the 1980s. He told me that the boys would tell ghost stories about this particular building.

The motel sign in front of the office, used to glow neon in the night. The sign hasn't been lit up for some time and the office was nearly burned down in early 2018.

Originally established as a neighborhood grocery store, it eventually became a surplus outlet store. Today, only parts of the signs are still on the building and the doors are covered with bars and boards.

Despite being empty and covered in graffiti, the Schlitz beer sign still hangs outside this West Bottoms building, untouched by vandals.

Dock doors to abandoned KCK warehouse.

Sitting empty for a few years, the pool hasn't been used since Vivion Road YMCA was tore down. The pool was purchased, cleaned up, and reopened as a community pool in 2018.

Abandoned and overgrown bridge sits just feet from Cookingham Road.

Left: Sinks left all over the floor in the science classroom at Marlborough Elementary.

Below: Closed in 2015, the gymnasium at the Universal Academy Islamic School was still in really good condition.

Right: "We are the world" mural is starting the crack and peel. Hallway at Marlborough Elementary.

Below: Lockers left open, some with papers and books inside at the Universal Academy Islamic School.

Left: Tape recorder left on a desk at the Universal Academy Islamic School. Teaching Islamic studies in addition to the basic curriculum for grades K-12.

Below: Abandoned trailer left under a bridge in the West Bottoms.

Inside the concession area for the I-70 Speedway.

Behind the businesses of Southwest Boulevard and beyond the railroad tracks, Imperial Brewery sits slowly falling apart.

Playground equipment left behind closed school.

Office and equipment keys left behind in abandoned KCK warehouse.

Abandoned house in the woods.

While exploring abandoned places, it is not unusual to see one room completely trashed and destroyed, while the next room can remain untouched.

The center building on the motel property was the only part that was more than one floor at 4 Acre.

Many told their stories of their summer job at the arcade/waterslide, while others talked about how rough it was to slide down the concrete slide. Today it is covered in graffiti from the bottom to the top and trees are growing though the many cracks.

Lead paint peeling off the walls in hallway of Greenwood Elementary.

Inside the pool room at the Ramada. In addition to lots of furniture and trash being thrown into the pool, a pick-up truck was found in the pool. (Truck not pictured.)

Carousel slide projector left on the desk in the science lab at the Universal Academy Islamic School.

Staircase leading up to warehouse locker room in KCK abandoned warehouse.

Part of the dinosaur mural in the hallway of Marlborough Elementary.

Classroom at Marlborough Elementary.

Left: Ceiling falling in on this office in abandoned KCK warehouse.

Below: One of the small cottages at the 4 Acre Motel.

Ropes still hanging in the gym of Greenwood Elementary.

Ropes still hanging in the gym of Marlborough Elementary.

Above: Ropes still hanging in the gym of Paul Robeson Middle School.

Left: Ropes still hanging in the gym of Attucks Elementary.

5

THE UNIVERSAL AVENUE RAMADA

I never had a personal attachment to any particular abandoned building until 2016. The Universal Avenue Ramada had many names before and after becoming the Ramada, but it will always be the Ramada to me. The hotel had served the city for decades, but I had never been there until 2012, when I attended a local horror movie convention. The following years, I would go on to make so many friends that after awhile it became a family reunion.

The owner abandoned the hotel and left the country in late summer 2016. Since then, we have gone on to find a new location for the festivities; however, there will always be a special place in my heart for where it all began. That part will always be saddened of what became of our hotel. The hallways where friendships began, the stage where I stood to get married, and the malfunctioning elevator all looked like they survived a war zone. After two fires, the discovery of two dead bodies, and the countless scrappers and vandals, the city had it demolished, leaving a vacant lot.

Front lobby of the Ramada Inn on Universal Avenue. Photo taken days after the owner left the country, abandoning the hotel in late October 2016.

The breakfast area at the Ramada. One week after being abandoned in late October 2016.

Ramada front lobby a couple weeks after being abandoned. Photo taken November 2017.

That same breakfast area at the Ramada. Photo taken in November 2017.

The Ramada hotel bar completely trashed a little over a year after being abandoned. Photo taken in November 2017.

Hallway leading to the ballroom, pool, bar, and breakfast area of the Ramada. Photo taken in November 2017.

While many of the buildings I venture into have been empty for years, even decades, the Ramada's days were numbered the day it was abandoned. Over a year and a half, I photographed the rapid decay of this nine-story hotel. My first time returning was a week after it was abandoned. Everything was oddly pristine. Beds were still made. Housekeeping carts were left in the hall, as if someone was cleaning close by. The front desk was left ready for the next shift to take over, not knowing their's would be the last.

Another week later, I went back. It only took two weeks after being left for the destruction to begin. It was such a shock to see what a week could do. Everything of value was stripped. The pool was full of beds and other furniture. The hallways were left unrecognizable. It was exactly like an animal carcass in the desert being picked apart by the vultures. Only the bones left behind. From that visit on, it became about documenting the rapid decline. With all the other places I've been, they were already abandoned or destroyed.

This was the first time I watched it from beginning to end. From the moment it was left for dead to the rubble cleanup after it was imploded.

Vandals leave the exit sign hanging from wiring after tearing down the ceiling. Photo taken in November 2017.

Arcade game moved from the first floor to the fourth floor. This must have been difficult bringing it up all those stairs, since there was no power to the hotel.

Destroyed elevators at the Ramada hotel. Photo taken in November 2017.

Above: Fourth floor view of the pool, just a little over a year later. Photo taken in November 2017.

Right: A year after being abandoned, the Ramada is a far cry from the hotel it used to be. All the windows are gone. Trash and destruction around every corner. The hotel would be imploded seven months after this photo was taken.

6

ST. FRANCIS SERAPH CATHOLIC CHURCH

Another abandoned place that is no longer standing is St. Francis Seraph Catholic Church. Formally located in the East Bottoms, when first built, the original church started off modest.

The bigger church was rebuilt in 1924 by its own parishioners and the renovations over the years would eventually go on to include a school. Opening in 1941, the last class graduated in 1962.

After closing, the school was sold off. The church would continue to serve its congregation until the doors closed in 1991. After that, St. Francis Seraph would sit empty for decades until it caught fire in August 2018, leaving a hole in one of the city's oldest neighborhoods, and the former students and members with just their memories.

There weren't many rooms to St. Francis Seraph Church. Besides the main worship room, there was only a small office and bathroom in the back and a choir balcony above the front entry doors. The back rooms were torn up badly. I only knew it was a bathroom because the sink was still partially attached to the wall. The ceiling was beginning to decay from the years of roof leaks. In the basement, the church pews were all stacked up. Some had been moved, but looked untouched for the most part. Surprising enough, although missing pieces, you could still make out the designs on the stained-glass windows. After the fire, I had hoped to photograph the shell of the church, but it was completely leveled days after the fire.

Right: Once located in the East Bottoms at the corner of North Agnes and Martin Street was St. Francis Seraph Church.

Below: St. Francis Seraph Church's cornerstone. Dated 1924.

View from the choir balcony at St. Francis Seraph.

Entrance and choir balcony at St. Francis Seraph.

Above left: Ouija board left behind from another person's previous visit to St. Francis Seraph.

Above right: The church's stained-glass windows are all missing pieces, but designs can still be made out.

Right: View of stained-glass windows from outside St. Francis Seraph Church.

7

PAUL ROBESON MIDDLE SCHOOL

Not all abandoned places in Kansas City go on to have a tragic end. Many empty schools all over the city have been into converted into lofts, and affordable and senior assisted living, including Horace Mann, Old Faxon, and Switzer. However, for Paul Robeson Middle School, the plans are very different.

Built in 1960, the school that would become known as Paul Robeson would see many changes over its lifetime. Originally a Jewish Community Center, the Kansas City Public Schools bought the property sometime in the 1980s, but didn't convert it into a school until 1990 when it became a Greek magnet school. After declining enrollment, it became Paul Robeson Middle School in 1998, until it closed in 2004.

Courtyard entrance to first floor main common/office area and library patio on the second floor at Paul Robeson Middle School.

Damaged hallway with exposed piped at Paul Robeson Middle School.

Science classroom at Paul Robeson Middle School.

Vandalized classroom at Paul Robeson Middle School.

Of all the places I have explored, Paul Robeson is my favorite school. Having visited there a total of four times, every trip produced new results. A treasure trove for urban exploration, there are hidden places at every turn. The nearly 152,000-square-foot school includes tunnels under the auditorium seating and stage leading to the green room and dressing rooms set up for the drama department, two racquetball courts with an overlooking balcony, a gymnastics practice area with some remaining equipment, and an Olympic-sized swimming pool. The climbing ropes were also still hanging in the gym. The school is so big that the first couple times there, I retraced my steps by remembering room numbers to ensure I knew where a definite exit was. After that, so many entrances were made that you didn't have to remember the way in.

Tunnel from the back of the projection room, running under the auditorium seating and stage at Paul Robeson Middle School.

Above left: View from diving platform from the pool at Paul Robeson Middle School.

Above right: View from the shallow end of the pool at Paul Robeson Middle School.

Open side entrance to the auditorium at Paul Robeson Middle School.

Now, after sitting vacant for well over a decade, projected plans allow the versatility to carry over from the school days into the future. Plans include a recreation center, child care facility, a retail area, and a senior living community. Paul Robeson can once again be utilized for a wide variety of people and the community at large.

Bleachers in the area for gymnastics at Paul Robeson Middle School.

8

THE NORTHEAST RESERVOIR

On the complete opposite of the spectrum, the Northeast Reservoir is also abandoned, but as of March 2018, no plans have been announced for what the future holds. The Northeast Reservoir was built in 1920 and held sixteen-million gallons of water for industrial businesses operating in the area. A combination of pressure cracks draining the reservoir and an improved facility being built to meet the increasing demand left the reservoir abandoned in 1931.

Today, the reservoir sits high atop a hill surrounded with by a wrought-iron fence within Kessler Park and Cliff Drive Scenic Byway. Trees and bushes grow out of the cracks and wall seams. Graffiti covers the floors and walls inside the reservoir. The two towers that sit on each side of the center wall still stand there. The ladders are rusted, and the concrete platforms are crumbling from years of weathering. The Department of Parks and Recreation has asked the local community for ideas for the reservoir, but nothing has come to fruition.

Standing outside the wrought iron gate of the Northeast Reservoir.

Overgrown trees block a complete view of the Northeast Reservoir.

Left: Graffiti and trees cover the inside of the reservoir.

Below: View of center walkway and tower inside the Northeast Reservoir. Center walkway separates the sides of the reservoir.

Above: Looking up the ladder of the tower in the reservoir.

Right: No trees to block the winter time view from the center walkway in the reservoir.

9

JOHN K. STARK SCHOOL

Another place with current plans is John K. Stark School. Plenty of history can be found about the school's namesake; however, after 1966, little to no information can be found.

I was able to locate a letter from the 1961 school principal, William Barber, detailing the history of the purchase of the school land in 1927, the cornerstone ceremony in 1930, and the growing pains that John K. Stark experienced when first becoming a school. Enclosed was a letter listing of all the principals from 1930 to 1966. After that, I was unable to find a definitive reason as to the why and when of its eventual closing. In 1977, Tri-City Baptist Church bought the Stark school, turning it into a private school. Tri-City Christian School taught junior and senior high school.

Above left: Main entrance to John K. Stark.

Above right: Paint curls off the wall in the first-floor hallway at John K. Stark.

Right: John K. Stark is in bad shape due to vandals and weathering, the scoreboard is surprisingly in good condition.

Second floor hallway and stairs covered in graffiti at John K. Stark.

Vandalized lockers moved from the hallway into a class at John K. Stark.

I managed to get in contact with a couple of former students that attended the Christian school from 1993 to 1998. No one I spoke to could confirm if Stark closed in 1966 or when Tri-City's moved out of the Stark building.

Getting into Stark wouldn't be nearly as difficult as locating information. Behind the school, there was clothing thrown all over the ground leading up to the back door. The three-story school still had the first Corinthians bible verse on the wall of the gymnasium. School assignments were scattered everywhere. Lead paint has cracked and curled off the walls, while other parts of the plaster walls have fallen off, exposing the inside frames. Orange sets of lockers have been either overturned or moved from the hall into classrooms. The cafeteria hardly had a ceiling. Stalactites were forming on the metal framing of the ceiling due to years of water falling through.

In all my looking for information about the school, besides the condemned structure notice on the front door, I couldn't find information regarding any future plans for the structure.

School assignments cover the floor in this classroom at John K. Stark.

Back entrance into John K. Stark School.

Above: Most of the Corinthians bible verse still hangs on the gymnasium wall at John K. Stark.

Right: This sign is a futile effort.

10

THE I-70 SPEEDWAY

The I-70 Speedway, while located just outside of the city, was a longtime Kansas City institution.

Opening season began in 1969, and this asphalt round track would go on to host races with all kinds of drivers, from amateur to some of NASCAR's greats. I can only speculate as to why the track closed in 2008, but from the figures and information found, it appears that an oversaturation of race tracks in the Kansas and Missouri region, in which half of those are within 100 mile proximity of the Kansas City area, would be the beginning of the end.

I managed to squeeze in two visits to the track. The first trip was before it was recently purchased. Trees were growing up through the spectator seats. The snack bar and announcers' box was completely trashed. Heavy equipment and old school buses were left scattered throughout the property. The once brightly colored finish line was now faded and chipping away. The 110-octane fuel pump was still sitting in the center of the track, next to the pit area. I wouldn't get quality time on the track until my second visit. However, shortly before my return trip, the track was purchased.

The second visit would show off the progress being done for its grand opening as a dirt track in 2019. The seats and bleachers had all been removed for brush clean-up. The concessions and announcers' box was completely gutted to make way for renovations. This time, I walked the track and it was really cool to experience, even if on foot, how steep the incline really is.

Walking back to the road to leave, I knew that was the last time I would see the track as asphalt.

View from the middle of the track's steep incline at the I-70 Speedway.

Bleachers and concession/announcers box sit damaged and overgrown with trees at the I-70 Speedway. Photo taken February 2018.

Left: 110-octane gas pump in pit area in the center of the track at the I-70 Speedway.

Below: Chairs and trees removed from the bleachers and concession/announcers box completely gutted at the I-70 Speedway. Photo taken November 2018.

11

THE HISTORIC 18TH AND VINE DISTRICT

History runs deep through the veins of Kansas City. One of those places within the heart of KC is the historic 18th and Vine District. This neighborhood is home to some interesting African-American history. Going into these places, I thought I knew their histories. But what I knew was only a few details compared to what I would learn about this half-mile radius of town.

All within walking distance of each other, the next three places are part of my early stepping stones into urban exploration.

THE VINE STREET WORKHOUSE CASTLE

The Vine Street Workhouse Castle has sat abandoned for nearly fifty years. Constructed for the purpose of jailing for debtors while they worked off what they owed, the castle was completed in 1897 with the stones that were mined by the castle's own prisoners. The jail finally closed in 1924 and after many futile efforts to reuse the castle, it was deserted in 1972. Since that time, it has been overtaken by vandals and the deterioration of this historic landmark continues.

The graffiti is a constant at the castle. It is always different, but always there. The wood beams within the turrets are rotting away and falling in on each other. There are doors going up the tower; however, there are no stairs to get to the doors. The rooms are big and open with no roof. Trees have sprouted up and have been growing throughout the castle.

Street view of the Vine Street work castle.

Above left: Many trees are growing inside the castle and the stone walls are always covered with some kind of graffiti art.

Above right: Open doorways up the smaller turret show off the old wooden beams inside at the top of the turret.

There has been recent interest to save the castle by making it into offices; however, in my line of work, it is not unusual to read about abandoned locations finally being sold and having work begin, only to be empty and back on the market some time later.

Wheatley-Provident Hospital

No matter the outcome of the castle, it will always be a part of Kansas City's rich history. Another chapter to that history is about Wheatley-Provident Hospital, Kansas City's first black hospital. Historically my favorite, this hospital would go on to set precedent for the medical and African-American communities.

Wheatley began from humble means in 1902. It started as educational program for African-American nurses as well as doubling as a small hospital.

Despite being small and segregated, Wheatley would achieve educating and employing all black nurses, staff, and doctors. Wheatley would have the first hospital ward for children in the country at that time, setting the foundation for pediatric care today. It wasn't until 1918 when the hospital was renamed from Perry Sanitarium to Wheatley-Provident Hospital. Serving the community until 1972, Wheatley closed due to a newer facility being built less than a mile and a half away.

Front view of Wheatley-Provident Hospital.

Biggest room of the side wing added on after the hospital expanded to include a children's ward.

On my visit to Wheatley-Provident, we could only go through part of the building, because structurally it was not safe. The floors were badly decayed and falling though. The rest of the building wasn't much better. Graffiti covered all the walls, clothes and other personal belongings were left behind, and disturbingly enough, there were naked cabbage patch dolls laying all over the floor upstairs.

The hospital was purchased in the summer of 2018, in hopes of preserving and repurposing the building.

Above: Naked cabbage patch dolls laying all over the place on the second floor.

Right: Staircase inside Wheatley-Provident Hospital.

The walls of Wheatley-Provident are either vandalized or falling apart, exposing the original brick walls.

Attucks Elementary

Just a couple blocks away from both the Vine Street Workhouse Castle and Wheatley-Provident Hospital is another cornerstone in Kansas City's and African-American history. Attucks Elementary was named after Crispus Attucks, a black soldier killed in the Boston Massacre during the Revolutionary War. The school was established in 1893, but wouldn't move to its current location until 1905. The oldest standing black school in Kansas City, Attucks' original architecture would not include a gymnasium and auditorium until 1922.

After an exhausted search, I was unable to locate an exact closing date. Only a few references were made to it being empty for "over fifteen years." The years of neglect were abundantly clear walking through the school. The auditorium ceiling was caving in, the wood gymnasium floor was stripped down to the support beams, and all the classrooms were in sad shape.

Right: Front entrance of Attucks Elementary.

Below: Top of the stairs view of the front entrance of Attucks Elementary.

The ceiling is collapsing in on the auditorium at Attucks Elementary.

Auditorium seating at Attucks Elementary.

Despite the extensive damage throughout the whole building, paintings of children on the wall were still waiting at the end of the hall to greet you. And the climbing ropes were still hanging up in the gym. Walking around, it was a shame to see such history left boarded up to rot from the inside out.

As of March 2018, Attucks was sold with plans of making it a center for the arts. Driving by it since the purchase, fencing has been placed all around the school, every window has been replaced, and a few dumpsters were full of gutted building materials.

This leaves me feeling bittersweet. The bitter part comes from the urban explorer part of me, as there would be no more return trips to photograph the latest condition. The story I tell about abandoned Kansas City ends the moment someone decides to give these places a second chance. On the other hand, it is sweet to see necessary improvements being made for the surrounding community.

Classroom deteriorating over time inside Attucks Elementary.

Painting of children on the wall at the end of the second-floor hallway at Attucks Elementary. At first view down the dimly lit hallway, the painting kind of startled me.

Old school chairs left at the end of the hallway in Attucks Elementary.

The more these stories unfold, the abandoned parts of Kansas City read like a choose-your-own-adventure book. The building you pick determines the outcome. Uncertain fate? Succumb to some form of destruction? A new beginning on the horizon?

A surge of activity over the last couple years has woken what was once dormant. No longer left to sit in their poor conditions, much of abandoned Kansas City will be rejuvenated for new endeavors. And the places that can't be saved or reused are now gone, only leaving behind reflections from elementary schools, the remembrances of church gatherings, and recollections of what these places had to offer.

As an urban explorer, the recent decline in places around abandoned Kansas City does not worry me, because this is only a small part of the story in this ongoing adventure. Places will come and go. That applies to the occupied as well as the abandoned.

Back view of Imperial Brewery.

Above: Long view of the Hillside motel. Photo taken in January 2018. City had it torn down in February 2019.

Left: View down the long building of motel rooms at 4 Acre.

View from the third-floor landing. Once full of families, children playing, neighbors and friends hanging out in the courtyard, now Chouteau Court is quiet and empty.

Located on a hill high above the Armourdale and Argentine neighborhoods is Sauer Castle. Over the years, work that has been done is always torn up by vandals. Today the house is surrounded by high fencing and protected by guard dogs. No recent work has been done and the house continues to fall into a deeper state of decay.

ABOUT THE AUTHOR

Regina Daniel received her first camera before the age of ten. From that gift, her passion for photography was born. While on her path of turning that passion into a craft, Regina discovered urban exploration. That discovery would inspire a photo journey to visually immortalize the remnants of what the city leaves behind for bigger and better pursuits.

Regina started and operates Red Vixen's Photography, where she also specializes in architectural and cityscape photography, traveling outside Kansas City when possible. However, she always finds herself feeling like a tourist in her own hometown by finding some new part of the city to photograph.

BIBLIOGRAPHY

Alcock, A., "Abandoned Kansas City Hotel Set for Demolition at Taxpayer Expense", KSHB 41 Kansas City Online, June 8, 2018.

Barber, W., "History of John K. Stark School," Personal letter from school principal. October 24, 1961.

Black Archives of Mid-America, "History of Wheatley-Provident Hospital."

Bushnell, M., "Filled: The Real Deal on Northeast's Reservoir," *Northeast News Online*. March 14, 2012.

City of Kansas City, "City Sells Former Crispus Attucks Elementary School; New Development Will Anchor the East End of the 18th & Vine District," City of Kansas City News Release. March 1, 2018.

Collins, R., "KCMO Church on List of City's Most Dangerous Buildings Goes Up In Flames," WDAF-TV Fox 4 Online, August 9, 2018.

Collison, K., "Kansas City's First Black Hospital Is Saved Thanks to Redevelopment Deal," KCUR Public Radio. July 16, 2018.

Goodwin, S., "Kansas City Businessman to Restore Pair of Iconic Local Racetracks," WDAF-TV Fox 4 Online. July 18, 2018.

Gross, S. M., "Residents Scattered After Kansas City, Kansas, Affordable Housing Complex Closed," KCUR Public Radio. December 23, 2015.

Gross, S. M., "Gas Explosion Guts Part of Shuttered Housing Project in Kansas City, Kansas," KCUR Public Radio. April 29, 2016.

Honig, E., "What is That? Kansas City's Vine Street Castle," KCUR Public Radio. July 24, 2014.

Kansas City Parks & Recreation, "Kessler Park."

Kansas City Public Library, "The Pendergast Years: Kansas City in the Jazz Age & Great Depression, Saint Francis Seraph Catholic Church (First)," Missouri Valley Special Collections, Kansas City Public Library. SC30-8A, Box 4, Folder 7, #44.

Lawson, B., "Taste & See: First Black Hospital in Kansas City Left to Decay," KSHB 41 Kansas City Online. March 6, 2018

Martin, D., "Tri-City Ghosts: School Vouchers Raise the Possibility of Diverting Money into Abusive Faith Communities," The Pitch Online. March 7, 2017.

McGonigle, P., "Two of Kansas City's Oldest Buildings Near 18th and Vine Getting New Life," WDAF-TV Fox 4 Online. August 27, 2018.

Missouri Department of Natural Resources, Historic Preservation Program, Missouri Historic Building Inventory Form, Page 166 of 714, May 1992.

Newill, C., "The 8th Street Tunnel is a Gateway to Kansas City's History – But You Probably Can't Get In," KCUR Public Radio. September 15, 2016.

Pepitone, J., "Moldy Mess Found at KC Apartment Complex Could Force Out Tenants", WDAF-TV Fox 4 Online. September 9, 2014.

Roberts, B., "Roaster's Block Redeveloper Will Convert School into Mixed-Use Rec Center," *Kansas City Business Journal.* April 19, 2018.

Rothfield, A., "KCPS Has Plans for Former Ladd and Marlborough Elementary Schools," KSHB 41 Kansas City Online, October 25, 2016.

Spencer, L., "Plans Move Ahead for Art Center and Chinese University in Empty School at 18th & Vine," KCUR Public Radio. December 21, 2018.

Strickland, M., Lawson, B., "Taste & See KC: Abandoned Kessler Park Reservior," KSHB 41 Kansas City Online. March 9, 2018.

United States Department of the Interior National Park Service, National Register of Historic Places, NPS Form 10-900, "Attucks School." Pg. 2-6.

United States Department of the Interior National Park Service, National Register of Historic Places, NPS Form 10-900, "Lincoln High School." Pg. 22.

United States Department of the Interior National Park Service, National Register of Historic Places, NPS Form 10-900, "Spofford Home for Children," Pg. 18.

UNKNOWN., "Making Good Men at M'Cune Farm: Work of Institution Told at Cornerstone Laying," *The Kansas City Journal*, November 28, 1909.

Vaupel, A., "KC Hotel Owner Abandons Property; Demolition Could Cost $1.5M", *Kansas City Business Journal,* August 23, 2017.

Walters S., "I-70 Speedway Reopening in 2019 as a Dirt Track," *Racing News* Online. August 3, 2018.

Willoughby-Roos, R., "An Eerie Tunnel Offered Greenwood Elementary Kids Safe Passage Under Busy KC Intersection," *Kansas City Star* Online, October 29, 2013.